Species

Species
Mark Burnhope

ISBN: 978-0-9927589-2-9

Cover photograph © Eleanor Bennett
www.eleanorleonnebennett.zenfolio.com

First published June 2014 by:

Nine Arches Press
PO Box 6269
Rugby
CV21 9NL

www.ninearchespress.com

Printed in Britain by:

imprintdigital.net
Seychelles Farm,
Upton Pyne,
Exeter
EX5 5HY
www.imprintdigital.net

Species

Mark Burnhope

Nine
Arches
Press

new poets series

Mark Burnhope is a poet, editor and disability activist born in 1982. He studied at London School of Theology before completing an MA in Creative Writing at Brunel University, London. His work has appeared in various magazines and anthologies in print and online, as well as two previous chapbooks: *The Snowboy* (Salt Publishing, 2011) and *Lever Arch* (The Knives Forks and Spoons Press, 2013). Mark co-edited *Catechism: Poems for Pussy Riot* (English Pen, 2012) with Sophie Mayer and Sarah Crewe, and *Fit to Work: Poets Against Atos* online (launched April 2013) with Sophie Mayer and Daniel Sluman, books which won a Saboteur Award and the Morning Star Award for Protest in Poetry consecutively. More recently, he became co-editor of *Boscombe Revolution* alongside Paul Hawkins. Mark can be found living in Boscombe, Dorset, with his wife Sarah, four stepchildren, two geckos, a greyhound and, occasionally, one or two stick insects or mantids. *Species* is his first full collection of poems.

CONTENTS

'The law given by Moses is usually distinguished into three species: moral (treating of morals or of perpetual duties towards God and our neighbour); ceremonial (of the ceremonies or rites about the sacred things to be observed under the Old Testament); and civil (constituting the civil government of the Israelite people).'
   – **Francis Turretin (1623 -1687),**
   Institutes of Eclenctic Theology

'But naturalists are now beginning to look beyond this, and to see that there must be some other principle regulating the infinitely varied forms of animal life.'
   – **Alfred Russel Wallace**

'We will now discuss in a little more detail the Struggle for Existence.'
   – **Charles Darwin,** *The Origin of Species*

THE CLOBBER SHOP

You got it buddy: the large print giveth,
and the small print taketh away.
  – Tom Waits

Welcome, welcome. As you can see
we are well-situated in this passage,
slotted between civic court (earth)
and sentence (heaven). Second-hand
department store cum organic deli
(specialists in the ripest fruits).
Our vintage clobber flaps
in door-breeze and character; let me draw you
to the plaid shirt on the first hanger:
belonged to one whose head still fills the collar
(breath on a bottle-lip shrilling a note)
and frills on the sleeves! The charmer
minced through all the townsmen.
There, a pair of trousers filled by a man
of short stature (a leg will lift if you're lucky);
wandered the city for scraps
and issues to sell, as he saw the poor doing:
study, and you'll see crumbs
the length of the pleats. (Amuse yourself!
Once, while he scrounged,
a wire-wool man preached the street,
clutching bible to chest
like Moses his commandments.)
So, to our most fabulous rack,
carrot to our tourists' ass:
The ex-military-man who wore this dress

passed in ecstatic state, but
her demeanour shimmers in the star-glitter
shocking the sky-like bodice.
There, the souled plimsolls of a girl
who faced cruel-unusual in the school
shy of this shop, their tongues tied
tight as their laces, tiny lashing-belts (so
I'd keep my mitts to myself if I were you).
Careful: *Fragile*. Don't trip on those boxes
brought to us by charity workers: lowered
down before they wiped their foreheads,
washed their hands.

Now, what interests
you about this post,
or were you hoping
to give a garment a spin?

THE SPECIES THAT BEGAT THE BINARIES

I

The Moral is a magnificently resilient mammal:
both natural / unnatural, and neither, thanks
to its ability to buck the competition rider
off its saddled back.
      Police and Paralympians owe much
to its domestication, the increasing rarity
of its wild-stampede ways of working.
If it's allowed
to run in herds today,
there will usually be a cowboy lasso nearby e.g.
man shall not ride with a man (beast)
as with a woman (burden).

II

The Ceremonial is a beautifully elaborate bird:
both natural / unnatural, and neither, thanks
to its clown-plumage being both of feather
and watercolour paint.
      Passengers and fanciers owe as much
to its evolution, and the progressive science
of its flight, as to an eaglet's first fall
from a cliff-side,
      finest impulse for further research.
For every flock or fleet flying today there will be
a mother, or mothership, setting the pace e.g.
blind, lame, disfigured, deformed with a crippled foot or hand,

hunchback; no dwarfs, eye defects,
         festering sores or damaged testicles.
    No high priest (beast) may
offer gifts with any defect (burden).

III

The Civil is a graciously disobedient invertebrate:
both natural / unnatural, and neither, thanks
to the Year of Jubilee made for it. It makes no
bones.
MPs and dissenters owe as much
to all of its landmine-grey intersections
as to its pulp-innards, pulsing as a single
muscle propels
              an exoskeleton of identities.
In every constituency, the sting of its abdomen
is bottled as antivenin, injected into guinea-
pig skin, and driven
              on rioter-occupied roads e.g.
at the end of every seven years, you (beasts)
must cancel all debts (burdens).

"Am I Disabled?"
– A Self-diagnosis Questionnaire

Be advised: this questionnaire should not
be used instead of a medical diagnosis
but as a companion to it. The medical field
has meticulously written your synopsis
step-by-painstaking-step.
We have no intention to tread on their toes,
accidentally or otherwise.
The purpose of this questionnaire is to flesh
out your narrative, just enough for you
to begin
to break
through the fourth wall – 'come out,' if you will.

1. Do you ever feel destabilised, in life and / or limb?

2. Do you have a car you struggle to:
      a) pay for yourself?
      b) dignify with a human name?

3. If you have a car:
      a) Do you tend to rely on the car in town?
      b) Do you look left and right before
      opening the door, thinking the worst
      kind of person could be stood there,
      demanding to see your credentials?

4. Do you miss the days when three-wheeled cars
could be seen regularly on the roads?

5. If you no longer have
regular sightings of three-wheelers, do you
have regular sightings of anything?

6. If you answered No to question five,
does this bother you?

7. If you answered Yes, does this
make you want to Salsa with somebody?

8. Do you wrestle with what your feet are for?

9. How long has it been since you last looked
between your toes and treated the inevitable build-up,
whether with concern or even contempt, and flounced
out of the room
leaving the fungal cream completely alone?

10. Does anything on your body uncontrollably:
      a) hang low?
      b) wobble to and fro?

11. How many names for knots can you identify
in a medical dictionary? (It doesn't matter
whether you could tie them.)

12. Can you throw over your shoulder:
      a) a tennis ball?
      b) a school satchel?
      c) a school teacher?

13. Remember that satchel: were you ever taught
how to recall the order of items
you needed to pack for the day?

14. The scenario: you've been called hero, soldier,
asexual attention-whore. But could you, when drafted
or backed into a corner and shafted, hold up in a war?

15. Do you give two hoots about who governs either
you, or:
      a) your immediate family and vicinity?
      b) your postcode / county / country?
      c) your soul on one level, the chronology
      of every Spatial frontier on another?

16. Do you always pronounce "bow" properly?

Taxonomical

We labelled aspects of our house
with collective nouns: idle of sofas, gleam
of lamps, sympathy of teaspoons,
as zoologists do.

When she left me, I willed every day
to scuttle back under the gravel, gathered
a grievance of takeout menus,
had a man fling a fold
of furniture into a van
                    and move me
to a flat in a town
overrun with one-man flats

wherein I released the idles, gleams,
sympathies, grievances, folds – resolved
to call the rest by my own names.

To My Kreeping Krypto-faith, Krampus

For December's festivities, dress yourself
(young man, queer-cripple, untermensch)
in the fur of some creature gifted the bullet
(sable-horned, cloven-hooved), the clothes
of growth's gradual epiphanies. From his lips
and teeth, hang a long-ribbon-tongue.

Your title drags the Christ
Mass through dust; combines grump, Gramps,
cramp, and pus (St. Paul's sprinter pulling
a calf, keeling over, footing a fierce blister).

Your name contains campus and hippocampus:
the civic space wherein they (re)formed us,
the brain-piece that converts short-term memory
into long, fosters spatial awareness. *Krampus*

Is An Evil Man, Vienna government wrote
in a propagandist pamphlet. But they lied.
Krampus is Lore. Nobody (only innocence)
died. Tonight, you shall get shit-faced
on schnapps, *that's me in the corner, losing
my religion* blaring from the bar behind you.

Tonight darkness rides the same sleigh as light.
So, do a runner without paying the tab
into the town you've been imprisoned in. To
help you navigate the side-streets bladder-eyed
summon Hel, queen of the underworld within you.

Swing your chains around your head; chase
down each child who looks like you did,
whipping their butts with bundles of ruten.
Frighten the fundamentals out of them.
Make the mountains tell of all you've done.

HUSBANDRY RESOLUTIONS

You, year, will be
a farm, and me
a farmhand.
I will corral and ring-fence
all of my elements.
                    I will in-
corporate animals into more
that I do, in so far as they
too are corporeal; they will still
command the same
        intellectual and emotional pull
as when I was five,
placing plastic livestock into piles.
My ground will erode slowly
into water: sedimentary rock, and all
        that silt.   Context
will no longer be prerequisite.
Can I save the whales, bottle
their sea,   MP3
their permissive moan?
Come, cock

        your ear.

Mallard, a Gentleman's Game

played with Ira Lightman

Bird drawn in

surreal unfettered

artistry by

an avantist

playing

snooker:

head   upholstered   green

collared in   clerical   high-class

white

pride
of England's ponds.

The cue

bursts

balls

then

all

over.

Body-brown

            breast-red

yolk-yellow

         struck

             along

                  the beak

     tapped-in black

chalk-cube-

        blue if   wings splay out.

Me old ducker   Ira –

        watch

        where   those get shot.

SERMON ON THE MOUTH

in praise of the white rhino

Let us never discuss
vastness, drag mass in,
before agility: the dust she
drums up when enraged
which whorls the muzzle,
whose width / colour
puzzles etymologists.

Imagine a mist, heat-haze:
when its own is in danger,
one able to conjure cloud
rivals the photogenic veldt;
a child won't be trafficked into
the city, tailor-maimed for duty-free,
if he bolts for her storm's eye.

Here is hope that hedges,
our guidebooks' promise.
Worry less of wideness than
the fibrous hairs it takes
to make one rhinoceros horn,
and the love made manifest
in any mother who bears one.

SILKY SIFAKA

Death and the wildlife documentary
have made me lemure-mad;
lemure meaning malevolent
larvaed spirit, *larva* meaning
not young mayfly
but mask; everywhere else
this soft eye-
white fleece.
His name is his cry's shapes.
He is the ghost of all our losses
treating trees as stepladders –
  even

   the unborn son
whom every family in this town
settles to watch on television,
living room windows
private as grief itself.
Good, for every night now I go
into my garden, throw black beans
from a polythene bag
    over my shoulder
to evoke, then dissolve my memories.
   They haven't found me
so far, touch wood, or those
prosimian congregations in the clouds.

fragments from THE FIRST WEEK
OF THE WORLD: THE HERPETOLOGICAL BIBLE

Day One

Smoke, and *the sudden mutism*
of the universe. Beginning
in your beguiling, *the agonising tautology*
of the common word: "Leopard."

Golden vessel
to swill night-light
    and day-dark,
take them into, and
   through
   the long vista of her torso
      to become *Gecko,*
splinter of horizon,
           chicken-pocked black:
           Earth refraining

from entertaining *the idea of death.*
She carries, and is carried. Pour one
     of a number
of substrates over the floor: *freedom,*

her bed and basking ground.
    At night, her four-footed name will grow
into its own: *Eublepharis macularius.*
The first day is good   nay, immaculate.

Day Two

Microcosm, coat-of-arms
for three separate seas:
Indian, Caspian, Arabian.

Imagine claws clapping the surf,
each a serrated head of an oar.
Second day. So little to say
for Leopards in water.

When she sheds
dead skin can cleave to foot, claw,
inhibiting circulation in the limbs.
Run a bath of maybe an inch.

Dip her, still in your hand, a minute.
Lightly pry away the skin
with fingernail, or cotton bud.
She'll never have been nearer water,

your fingers the breeze, the mull
around her toes of a mock-current;
she may suddenly seem at home.

Imagine: the captive-bred
recalling her surroundings,
closed in only by porcelain.

Day Three

The Leopard is lassoed
via crepuscular eyes,
stipple-pupils snagged

in a dragnet of stars.
You have screwed in
the UV light, created

new constellations, joined
the dots. *On. Off. On. Off,*
an indecisive Orion;

allowed her heat via
a mat lain across
a glass tectonic tray.

Day Four

There is sheep-sky, there is goat-ground,
and she: a toffee-wrapper on the ground.

There will be no binary anymore but *paper*
and *pen*. Such a zoology, friend, is sound.

We say she *split*, meaning not that a lemon
was sliced by a knife, but that she was found.

If we say this rescue-case was bred we mean
more than *emerged* when we say *crowned*.

There is mealworm, wax-worm, locust, cricket.
There is manna, flatbread, olive, skin and rind.

Day Five

A *crack* and a *shriek*. She flickers away.
Awakened from sleep, she flickers away.

A branch or a leaf, a bat or a bird.
The leopard is meek. She flickers away.

A wind in the brush, a *bray* in the herd?
A *step* and a *creep*. She flickers away.

The gathering guns a thorn in her side.
Unable to weep, she flickers away.

Afghanistan play. Afghanistan hide.
Afghanistan seek. She flickers away.

D( )y S( )x

Essay records epiphany
(Joyce's sense-word) – lizard
on the wall of a ruined house.

The prosaic perception
might confront: agonising
tautology (common word).

Sudden mutism,
idea-death, resort to
'freedom' within himself

(Rilke's transformation,
Heidegger's institution
of being the poet's part).

Bonnefoy speaks:
logos, universe, impulse
towards salvation.

The real 'interiorised',
inward search for 'threads
that unite *within me.*'

Day Seven

The seventh day. Your Leopard is at rest,
her arms and elbows folded out, her chin
on the substrate, a devout bowing down.

When all the building of her house is done,
you can almost hear her sing a bhajan
to a care-taker deity on the air:

Upon this rock your warmth finds me, Lord;
the gust of your robe as you go past my glass,
a bridal veil. I have to lick my eyes clean.

With every dig of a hole I will worship you.
When I burrow through a new tunnel
I will christen the distance: lesser-catacomb

to carry communities of praises. My eyes,
studded with pinholes filtering light,
will fix upon your wide-flung temple canopy.

I was a nomad once, never knowing where
to lay my head. You were the home-strait,
window and gate to end my wanderings,

now the substrate under these fingers.
Even my gold inheritance, silent crickets, spring
and scratch in their box a sort of song.

See your gecko bask and you may well
wonder whether, inside her frozen frame,
there is not something other going on.

Uromastyx, Desert Father

Roasting sands rustled him up a devil who said:
Tortoise-headed Egyptian, did humans cast you
out to where they fling scapegoat, road-kill, sin?

If you're starving, stamp the stones to mustard.
If you're so foot-sure, leap the ravine and land
on all-fours. Follow me: Man of Sun and Earth.

But Uro trampled the devil's appeals underfoot,
kneaded no stone (lizard cannot live on seed alone),
led his devil deep into thicker outcrops;

learned to skull and plunge the acacia shrub,
love the prickle-weave around his head; red fruit
over his mouth, teeth, papyrus-rough tongue.

TRI-COLOUR: THREE CHAMELEON POEMS

Epiphany

The rule of nature that says
flowers appear where someone passes
may apply here: pink camellia
stepping across   windowsill and pane,
some still poised in the bud

                    like tongues.

for Coraline

our grief
     shall be tiny

     like the shine
of a lime-
green leaf

slowly arriving,
     all her way feigning
               a flat fern
          swaying

a girl
suddenly full
of colour,   a
colourful girl

sometimes a shade
so dour
     it depresses the hues
in even the palest
     human epidermis

sometimes a blue
                    like liquid fire
this feeling we left
our fags in the car

but not for the smoke
for the drag
   of matchstick legs
      over a hot   slab of bark

the regret: we
should have said no
to the vet,   no

to the cremation
   no, just
send her back to us

in the six-inch box
she came to you in

Consider the Pygmy Chameleon

a scuff   of autumn leaf
on thumb   palm   wrist

a cathedral in a thimble
the least forest scaffold

lacking everything
but deficiency

nylon hull   tentatively called
ribcage   a breathing cave

of mouth   gullet   lung
each in its own   trinket-time

requires her tail to perform
a labyrinthine curl

she opens   two blue eyes
run   through one

WATER RAIL, WITH MOSES

She breaches warmer waters:
distorted kiwi, beak too short
and orange to be a curlew's;

wears a similar fibre-blend
of brown-tan feathers.
Her eyes are dabs of blood.

Moses' basket and blanket
appears in the rushes; she parts
a sea of them to meet him.

Her sharming startles his story
into fruition: gnat, fly, locust,
all in a day's plague

to this alien rail. She emits
a series of grunts followed by
a scarpering-piglet's squeal

ending in purrs of contentment
(for territorial claim, alarm
or announcement).

She dips for food and I am made
to remember manna, her mouth
a pillar of fire with a reed's girth.

To My Hydrocephalic Sister, Champa the Moon Bear

Asiatic Black-coated, white-moon-
brained, you have known the sun
drain light from and provide light
to your fur. I don't know you, but I stroke
the back of my head, this shunt-lump
inches above my neck and I'd like to think
I know the life that left you

then returned. Let me write you a letter
no more open than the keyhole
they cut to feed your shunt through.
Grant me the surgeon's exact access
even as my inadequacy, heavy
and humid as Laos air,
weight-bears on every word. My head

has an itch for which I'd die for a paw:
maybe, if resurrection and 'rebirth'
are worth rough-and-tumbling with,
then, in our own ursine hemispheres,
we both have, both did, both do
and the stream we host and swim through
sets and rises to meet us, looping.

ABNOMINATIONS

WHIPPER IN, LAD!

An abnominal for Andrew Philip, inventor of the form

When rapped hard, win;
Reap reward in lead and pen.

When hindered, ailed,
Plan and nail a wider reel.

Delphian piper, raid-warnin',
Draw and din nae-endin',

Wander deadened lane and land.
Render a pariah healed

In laden-heid, dry-heel,
Raw-pain hip, peripheral ill.

Ne'er drain a red drip.
Wear a plaid readin' *Dear Laird, help.*

Happier allied wi' a Philippian line,
Heir wi' heid laid in hea'en,

Heap, pile, lid all pride and peril;
Hae air enwrap and plane wi' hail.

Padre de Aidan, wee pearl; new deer
Leapin' adder, drywall, rail, alder. Ha!

Dine in wi' a lap dinner,
Dear winner – hill, hairpin, hame.

I Am Odd-Craven

An abnominal for David Cameron

A camcorder? Come on den Mr,
A dare: video me doon common.

Record me road on CD and DVD.
Deem, and re-deem me (in code):

Vocoid drone. O mon acrid Con-
Dem cad, median no one needed.

Carved in avarice, no' candid. Aidman,
Medic – no one I admire, or ever did;

A dad, canned in a manic cameo,
Dire comedian, a drier Avid Merrion;

No' even a canard, cod in a marinade,
Cider, caviar, anodic cadaver on a divan;

A dram, a drone, a doer, a nice idea,
An icon, an income, a divine invader.

I dreamed I danced in an anaemic void,
A revered deacon in a coma, near-dead.

I carried an I.D. card, read: *Never come
Near me! Advanced cancer!* Reader, no

Economic arena cried me, an avoider.
Amend me mind O Can-Do-Man! Amen.

Deviancy as God

An abnominal for David Gascoyne

A caved saying: dang dingoes dosing!
Vain dogs, ego-divas, edgy agony-codas

Did as David does: danced giddy, de-
Seeded. Ovid aced yogi's inane, aged

Voyage. Dived good, snagged a gonad,
Donor in a saved Degas-coven. Navy Dave:

Gay voice, no novice, delicious screed,
Envoy via avid disco-gods and devices:

Isis, Isis, Isis! End, End, End. Diane (ye say),
Even a cage goes Cubic under sand. Savvy?

Doice vita! Said nay and grace gave us grain.
Gained gander's voice, never-ending, egads!

Said: soy is no acid. Dos ado! Adios adagio;
Venus, sun, dead-gross adenoids – en garde!

Advance, canvas, vin, coinage, casino, cove.
Dada! Dada! Dada! Goo-goo y gaga, de Dios!

Candid deed, avenged virgin of Ganges, say,
A Cash-Cod in a sea o' dead-end scansion: God

Is not dead, nada can do it. So! Good day Dave,
Divine tales decanted say *no cyanide diagnosed.*

A Dab-Toothed Grin Virus

An abnominal for Sir David Attenborough

Brass adventurist as o' ages ago; rough abrader
Anti-egregious agendas; sooth-birder, birthroot

O' great ideas; agitator o' hunter and abattoir.
Genius. Our antennae didn't avoid his adroitness.

Attuned atheist: averse to, distrusting o', ignorance,
Servant o' endangered beasts and good hearts.

Even the trees, Arborvitae, grown-on,
Arranged high, round, strain to hear him read

His ideas. Dab-hand, devoted guardian-herder,
He bears gritted teeth to berg erosion.

No raving brother denies he's grinned as a teen
At the bird-name: *Great Tit*. He taught us it,

Didn't he? Attentive author, nature narrator,
Avant-gardist bare-riding giant tortoises.

I overdosed on our nineties TV stoats, badgers,
Anteaters raiding holes, sea otters (overdone).

That shit hasn't died. Those trends, traditions,
He set. Our revisionist brings a threat to bathos

In his bright irreverent demeanour. An adder but
No bite – nearer to god, and other gravid designs.

CREAKED ANIMUS

An abnominal for Maurice Sendak

Immerses audiences –
Acned-Kid and reared,

Insecure and irked: *me* –
In a damascene drama dressed

In a canine-ermine mask, and man!
Earns us a mum's dusk dinner.

Makes mean isms easier –
Endured amid karmic ideas,

Sees maniacs askance, kind
In a measured manner;

Sees madmen, menaces,
Medusas Skinned, creamed, rendered,

Cured: read 'em in diner menus
Reused in cakes and rice snacks.

A rare miner run amuck, drunk
In caiman-diced mud, sand-dune, cack;

Skewed ram, auk-eared re-namer, rare
Mad-keen inker – drum ruckus! –

American dad I mark and deem
Curse-eraser, Dream-mender.

Hurrah! Sober on Piranhas!

An abnominal for Sarah Harrison-Burnhope

Is she ur sunshine? Si! Oui.
She has been. Pin: *SHE'S ON*

HIS BRAIN upon our pier
In Narnian sun, san' an' shore:

Bus o'er here. Hop on!
Brap! Soar in brine-air.

Hair raisin-broon, airborne,
She's Asherah (or on a par). Hun,

Hear about no ruse or harassin'.
She's no pash or pair o' *(hush)*.

Us and our Ash S. run brash
Sessions parsin' beers, nosh,

An' passin' uproarious hours on
P.R.A.S herps, bro-biases. Bra-

Burner, a harbour-erosion sparin'
No borin' ennui, reason, erasure.

As a baboon, I rise an' praise her:
(Ass-o'er-ears, an un-hero opens).

Perusin' Spanish bar and brasserie,
Shine on, bonnie Urbanhippie.

Hereby Love Unpin

An abnominal for Evie-Lyn Burnhope

Our bubble, li'l blip,
Hyper-breve eerily born;

Envoy, eyehole, helper –
Be inhere, herein, unhere;

Heron, heroine, holy union,
Honeybee – V.I.P hip hopper;

Our hourly hyperbole,
Linen burn, very inner irony;

Love, lively in lieu o' hope –
Eloper in liver, lobe, loin;

Neverlore, nil, none, nope,
Noun, novel y oeuvre: *her*.

Our only open leyline: olive,
Orb, ore, phoney oven-bun!

On hill, on pier, I pine – pin–
Bonny, hill peony, li'l plover.

Proven open pore, pure prier,
Hyper, ripe. Reopen. Relive.

Unborn, uneven, unveil
Your verb, *yelp*.

JIB PRONGS JINNS SIR

An abnominal for Jón "Jónsi" Þór Birgisson

Þis   brig
      ninon jib;

         Þis   born ibis rib
         no brió bring rós iris

Þis   joss-gnósis
      bong-grin

         nó Þin jingo
         sorb orris nigrosin

         I join in Þis song o'
         gibbon-origin   *gó*

                  nó sin Þorn   nog
                  rosin iron   sign

         I join   bóÞ
         griss-n-bison

                  bóÞ
                  job-n-boss

                  bóÞ
                  son-n-biro in Þis song

                           ( )-n-( ) noÞing
                           rising norÞ

48

SEREPENTENT

Cling to the Genesis account and Satan once crawled, claws to the grass. At first light I crawl too, bottom-shuffle if doing the stairs. Sometimes I wonder if maybe I am a host for him, a carrier: so he is entwined in veins and arteries, yes, but also VP shunt invasively planted from my brain to journey's-end. I wear him in the bath, both a second-skin and an internal foreign object, buoyant, bottle-green. We are sin together. Neither breaches a purity boundary on his own. But I am torn: so our relationship is totally undesirable. But without my Shibari-brother, would I have been able to learn desire at all? Would I know how to make love, fuck well; tie my shoelaces with these dysfunctional cripple-fingers? When the apple felt as sweet on Eve's tongue as it had looked on Adam's eye, did she imagine the rosebud nipple of a submissive sister-bride, lady-missionary? Did she watch it bloom? David's psalm so often quoted: *taste and see that the Lord is...* evoking all of Solomon's plush main courses. Did God really say they must not eat...? What if a truffle grows in a landslide after a monsoon? May I never elect to devour – proactive swine to a pearl, mongoose vs. spitting cobra?

I Still Recoil at the Smell of Fast Mustard

A university friend and I were standing
and sitting, respectively (my wheelchair with me)
at the exit of what was then The Opera House
after a night out: 'Slinky' if I remember rightly.

It was blind-drunk and we were dark.

I forgot my fucking coat, my friend shouted,
ran back inside leaving me piling
pavement slabs inside my mind, to some
residual trace of euphoric-trance.

I'm hazy, but this lady ambled over
(from which club I couldn't see, only
that over the road
three of her girlfriends were giggling).

Obviously off her heels on pills
given her glassiness as she came nearer
and her struggle to figure out
where to place her feet on a flat surface,
a foal finding a stable stance after foetal.

Picking at a McDonald's paper bag
she ended her mysterious slalom to me
and slurred: *What's someone like you doing
out so late and clubbing? I never knew
you people went clubbing.*

She leant over (I remember
a white puffer jacket, but otherwise
nothing of what she looked like)
and asked: *Do you like Big Mac?*

put her left hand in the bag,
shook it around, lifted it out again
then (palm painted-dripping with food)

pressed everything over my face,
rubbing quickly left to right in the style
of Tango TV adverts at the time,

laughing and laughing and laughing,
shouting: *Have some Big Mac!*

I opened my eyes and she was gone.

It took seconds to tell my hair was wet.

I still recoil at the smell of fast mustard.

My friend came out of the club wearing his coat
and (I didn't mind, it was dark, and I loved him)
looked around the town and couldn't believe,
he said, the amount of makeup
some girls could get away with wearing.

Poem in Which I Try to Raise a Photograph from its Bed

It cannot remember how he clocked me
in the capacity-packed amphitheatre,
   but I can:
my lower vertebrae were broken
   like bread
     at birth
   so by the time I am five – and I am
here – you can put me down
as 'sick'
   according to first-century
Greco-Roman categorisation:
   that Spina bifida gait,
orthopaedic shoes,   crutches,
   a PV shunt scar   under all my blonde.
I've been fed to front of the queue
   at a few meetings, but this
is bigger, like reading the Braille of death
engraved into the inside metal
   of a gladiatorial helmet.
The man's suit is blue-grey
   as moral clout himself.
   He holds the microphone
as close to his chin
   as his chest,   surfaces
of vice   and workbench,
   my head, my whole personhood
     held between them.
This boy, me – dwarfing him
   as if about to receive
     an award, not a verdict –
knows he needs healing

and wears those colours;
    they will flap
        in his face   for years yet.

If you could see the front of me
    my eyes would be tightly closed.
The boy leans all of his faith
    against his crutches
        to tether his wilder inclinations
until such a time as their metal
    knows when   to let him go
        onto his heels,   his healing.

The spill of stage lights
    licks the vignette's skin
like pipetted   liquid,
        a serpent coiled round
            lady wisdom.
Some believers, this boy will learn,
        wrangle venomous snakes
every Sunday.   Whether
in colourful crowds of thousands
or pews of coughing,
        amen-throwing tens,
we all seek the same signs
and wonders, when 'God'
    might simply be
the commemoration of expectation,
        the photo – part
of a newspaper cutting my mother framed,
    probably in some attic now, suffering
        an invisibility
        like hell – enough
that both prayer and prayed-for know
power is left imperfect in her strength.

NOAH

for Jo and Sam
in memory of Noah Holdsworth
(28th Jan – 22nd Feb 2013)

After we'd floated
                     for forty days, it was settled:

the heart
              is the greatest ark, able

to house both light,
                 flight-feathered, and far-

too-heavy-to-bear.
                 Only as we disembarked

onto land,
             slowly retaught our feet

to negotiate
               the mountainside, and our eyes

to read the sky's
                magnificent arch,

had we begun to under
                   stand its buoyancy.

DUCKING THE QUESTION

This wooden stool
sunk into the bank
by hefty chains
heads a cobbled lane
called The Drum: to the touch
like a pew, I imagine.

Me and my wife, Sarah,
watched Ashley climb in
for a photograph;
our laughter drowned out
all the drunks in Ye Old George

whose own chains rattled
and groaned seconds ago
like the wax-worked on trial
for London Tower tourists

whose gasps and applause
rose and died with the triumph
over adversity cliché, a feather
blown about in austerity's cap.

*

Sarah stood at the stool's base,
told Ashley to smile, and I did
but they didn't clock me.
God, she suddenly beamed;

leaves shone like fists of money,
tree trunks were stakes snuffed out
in the cool stream. Hard patriarchy
lies under fathoms today.

She replicates, with wool,
the earth's patterns. Here is sorcery:
that she should untie her hands,
run on her way. Fuck the naysayers.

*

An ATOS assessor
was at the helm. I mean
I was in an interview room
with the wall-to-wall scrotes.

It is rumoured, the guy began,
you write poems thus can operate
a keyboard with ease: a bandit
cloaked by trees in a quiet verge

called Workshire; that you think
yourself something of a bard.
I would not hold your breath,
he said as he unloaded me.

*

I saw Ashley, then,
lowered in the long limb
till the prick saw fit
to raise him; felt

myself sat in that seat,
then sunk
to the queer intonation
of a judge's go;

to have to hold
a lungful before being lifted,
the scolding lasting
the time it took to deny my craft.

*

The centuries churned,
uncovered change; it glinted.
The Mill – for so is the body
of water now named – is shin-shallow.

A high street herbalist conjures,
heals his customers content.
My wheelchair couldn't
cross the grass so I didn't run

my hand over the contraption,
but we all felt it: tried
by the stool, a woman
committed to a cripple
committed to a gay friend

whom I remember smiled
and (finding the stool
unable to make
even a penitent creak)
pleaded *cheese*
to the charges.

STANDING IS THE APPLES TO SITTING'S ORANGES

On the Diamond Jubilee debacle
pink-suited Elton John sings:
I'm still standing but the thing is
he isn't. Note: the stool buckling under
his gravitas. Every band member stands
but the drummer, or everything before
the jam – cool, measured – is butchered.

Standing is staring, greenly, at the fence
Elton croons subliminally, bids me to climb
higher towards the heights he frequents,
employ unprecedented levels of sleeping
muscle. I rise from the sofa, open
the curtain, jot down our encounter's gist
as furiously, and frankly, as I can:

There is a morality in being able
to trouble the highest shelf
for platitudes and choruses,
to straddle the tallest trees for their fruit.
For every ladder man ascends to change
a spotlight, somewhere
a philanthropist spearheads an idea.

Even hurtling south has virtue: feeling
grass-blades bend beneath the balls
of one's feet, a green uprightness
in the chasms between one's toes.
They queue outside the venue, pilgrims
punctuating the festival's fertile banks;
and you'd settle for sitting ovations?

To My Parallel-Parked King, Richard III

Cheated of feature, deformed,
unfinished, we have called ourselves.
Hedgehog, bottled spider, foul bunch-
backed toad, diffused infection of a man,
we have been called by women
diluted in a playwright's quill and ink.
Now my names: planking skiver,
striver for naught but pity,
the perfect party-political binary.
Mark: for all the names they gave me
we may as well have been buried
beside ourselves: one cockentrice
(dry-cured, butterflied, fossilised)
to rule them all.
So many species of automobiles
came to a stop on top of us we could
be called scrap-yarded cars ourselves.
My King, I'm making a meal of it
but what I'm trying to say is this:
in our new new identity as vulnerable,
'difficult-to-place' claimants,
we have been royally parked
by tourism, media, leaders, law-makers,
powers greater than any of us
in our impotent states.
They mine our stone for money.
Even though your facial reconstruction
displayed chiselled-waxy planes
of the unmistakably-Charming, instead
of the gravid pores of the Surinam toad;

even though your scoliosis was found
to be mild, meaning little strain on arms
in battle (neither withered in any way),
yea, we can be reasonably confident
they have worked about us without us.
My family is an army in some manner
and our county of Surrey tested positive
for horse but they carry on being wrong
by half. My kinsman
in this farce (this farce),
I would have kept them from you if
I could have.

THE INNOCENTS: A FOUND POEM

I live in a country with a monarch, no constitutions,
and no guns. I have never felt safer.
  – Robert Peake, *Huffington Post,* 12/19/2012

Some say their significance is
that the messiah survived among them.

I like the idea that their massacre
might be a literary echo

of mass infanticides found
in the Old Testament. But to what end?

Perhaps one point is that the rulers of this world
will go to great lengths

to prevent the embodiment
of spiritual truth in the flesh

as it is often dangerous
to the established order.

Sometimes it disturbs the comfortable.
Sometimes it comforts the disturbed.

I don't think it is one thing, but some part of us
recognises it when we hear it, and always

when put into action, it results
in loving choices and support of a greater good.

Paralympic Lessons: the Atosonnets

for all my fellow disability activists

Preliminary #1

Ludwig Guttmann gathered them from the War.
You can gather yourself, go on holiday, watch

from abroad. Gradually learn best formations,
where to be stationed for the games' beginnings.
Explore L'Eixample. Enter La Sagrada Familia.

Suddenly see an *other sentimentality*. Remember being
younger, practising a divided loyalty:

Team GB / Spain, Team GB / Spain. The former
didn't qualify, fine; you cheered on the latter. You won't
know where to settle your chair here either.

Wheels will involuntary shriek as they negotiate
all of the temple's trembling surfaces. The holy

tree's arches rise to the first rung, and as Gaudi
planned, bend into pairs. Go with them into the air.

Preliminary #2

Don't write down the details. Enter the basilica.
Absorb its never-completely-straight preciseness.

A modern St. George looms from the far wall,
patron saint of England and Cataluña. Forget
conventional order, go there first. Find a place

under his tipping Easter-Island wooden face.
This lesson is smaller than could carry a building,

sorry. There's no other way to say it: you will be
allowed in free, with a carer. The government
acting as scaffold for this building is that sending

Spanish athletes out to grace the games.
Get patriotic, even for one second. The sunlight

glorifying these windows' blue mosaics, cutting
rounded shapes out of these cave walls, is yours.

Preliminary #3

Tensions binding the games will make you feel
you're being shown to the Olympic Family seats.

Your political paranoia will mean that every man
sounds like Cameron till you've seen their faces.
If a young boy reading a book looks at a pirate

and sees an athlete, that's his wisdom. Go in
immaturely restless, even as you light a candle

for every Atos victim, some children themselves.
Tolerate Coldplay during the closing ceremony,
random cavalry choirs, singing: *para, para para...*

Lift hymns. Some will try to disable you further
for it. Ignore: finally, impairment fills the sky.

With your seated soul-kid, say: *He has one leg,
he must be an athlete.* Hit the point dead-centre.

Quarter-Final

The sponsor controls the competition
but you control your own game.

'Game', 'match' and 'kick-about'
are all perfectly valid words for what
you do. 'Job' doesn't come into it.

If at first you don't succeed, adapt
your sport slightly.

If they want to send your chair
flying several feet in the air, take the tackle;
they can't disable you twice.

Never lose your determination. They don't
make prosthetic determinations.

You won't always get even; relax,
tell yourself you are already equal.

Semi-Final

Propel yourself forward and campaign.
The fight for equality isn't a sport but only

because they could never cut that
many medals, enough impromptu altars
to our victories. Take time off. Self-care.

Maybe the pressure of this 'legacy' façade
makes your brain balloon but it may burst

soon, let you sleep. Maybe Coldplay
didn't para… dice the closing ceremony
into as many tiny pieces as you said.

True, Atos bulldozes closer towards you
but your situation may improve such that

you can afford to play statistic again. Say
the red-button function's due to change.

Final

When the Paralympics end you may
do more than mourn the wheelchair

basketball scoreboard. Clearly it would be
raining this morning, wouldn't it? Global
warming, climate change, both terms

for what you are experiencing: symptoms
of the day after, the new autumnal paradigm.

Cold weather pains come in two instalments.
Apart from in your hands, hold your head
at funny angles from your television,

to keep any cerebral shunt black-outs at bay.
Console yourself: if you'd had to hear

the damn medal-awarding ceremony theme
one more time, you might be dead. Be glad.

Phantasmantia I: matins

Wandering Violin,
body all toothpick-

Stradivarius neck,
look at this trans-

parent vestment you've removed,
pressed flat, in the minutes since

you renounced its comforts. You
sloughed yourself whilst my back

was turned to the TV: Eugene
Tooms deliberately dislocating

his mutated limbs to inhabit
his latest prey-item's air vent

accompanied by Hitchcockian
plucked strings. He had entered

the professional's office just as
your habit, straitjacket, landed,

no hellfire to sate viewers' hunger
for justice. Behind, and before me

played the paranormal agency
of seventy-times-seven repeal.

EUNUCH

she braces her body,
a dromedary

for water, bed chamber
alive with sighs

curse this lengthening want
for an older night

desire, dispensation, devotion
a son – lack

marks
us of the clean, white cloth.

PHANTASMANTIA II: ONE SON

Bend to understand my dream
of a display between two green mantises

(in as much as common names describe –
my ID guides are gathering bluebottles,

warping in loft-damp). Everything breaks
out at my bedside, my wife asleep.

Female swipes with a scythe and male
negates her attack. I take to my chest

the aggressive specimen, in the womb
of my fist (having heard what can happen

to his head); try to retrieve her species
designation. Before I've splayed my palm

she vanishes in a paroxysm of pink petals
so only male is left – a lesser invertebrate

somehow than in his gesturing. Bend
to understand: I sit up, and a pulled

abdominal (Sarah waking, whispering:
you were a father as far as I'm concerned)

leaves me fully myself but
armed to the mandibles, winged, segmented.

FAITHFUL

Not the one who takes up his bed and walks
But the ones who have known him all along
And carry him in...
   – Seamus Heaney, 'Miracle'

Not the one whose daily bed bears his iniquities
Because it was made by a fine village craftsman,
Not a corporation.

Not the one who nails his hands to both
Stretcher handles, in case his friends try
Abruptly to tip him off.

Not the friends who, in the beginning, were sold
On his humour, bought his struggles, levelled
His militant / victim scales.

But the one who, if he can bank on gossip about
A blind man, comes unskilled in silver glossolalia,
And offers a clean hand.

A Creed for Miscarriers

I know why I had to go through
my shunt failure now, and beforehand
had to abandon driving lessons.

I know that when my surgeon reset
my cognition overnight, and God moved
over my waters, bellowed *let there be light*

and there was clinic light,
it was because you would move
into one type of eternal life.

I know that in those two hallucinogenic weeks,
when I could not tell my well-wishers
apart from machines,

when the ward walls opened to reveal
two cogs grinding their teeth together,
they were perfect pictures of my grief

and though your mouth would never
utter our names, I would become
intimately familiar with both of yours.

I remember the sequence:
mirror, signal, manoeuvre, and as a kid,
being backseat driver in my parents' car.

I know that when my dad
pushed my wheelchair towards me
at the end of my shunt failure stay

and because my memory was shot
I said *this isn't mine*, even though it was,
it was because you are not mine but must be

if I'm to begin finding again
means to move forward, un-
assuming son, daughter, both, and neither.

DELIVERANCE

No one can swear how it fell
into our hands. No one
  – Andrew Philip, 'The Ambulance Box'

I awoke tonight,
my bedside clock a white receptacle
bearing time's nick

bleeding out   to tell you:
this   delivery
fell through our door as well,
five weeks ago now.

Who can tell
who is next?
                    So, to respond
                    to the instruction slip I took
                    as an invitation:

after the wards and waiting rooms
                    I envisage a visit
to The Ship in Distress

where a punter in a white-sail vest
who's been losing weight for the amount

of time his wife has bled of late
faints over the bar,
                        spills a pint;

to his wife
who tips the Solent into a teacup,
                sees trade ships in

two cubes of sugar   sinking,
thinking   she'd trade all of her
possessions to have him here;

to a boy floating his boat in a bathtub
full to the brim with everlasting water.

We could find them, usher them in
from the callused   strip-lit street,
tell them

wait indoors for news about the tests
the Spirit carries out upon our waters;

spinning her fingers, stirring the foam-
tipped waves into a salve,
and folding our earthen bodies into the swell

to see what weight they bear,
                            set their course.

ADAM AND EVE IT

Adam, before the difference
of half a wishbone, was an androgyne. Before Noah
no rainbow fun
damentalists insist. Run

for shelter
from their agenda. Remember,
men can make a meal of the word; Male and Female
cuts like Knife with Fork.

Up the Clobber Passage

Sometimes as the evening goes in, I imagine
that when she is six or seven,
Sarah, in her Coventry estate,
answers the door to someone
who is not me, her mother, father, even real:
a sequined angel, who adorns her
in whatever the colours of grace are,
and is transfigured within her as she grows
into a prism that refracts the colours
into new and unspeakable corners.
Meanwhile, wherever I was then, men were
showing me how to pivot round an offender:
pushing a wheel more than twice
when the ball is nestled between your legs
is called a travel, and is illegal –
do everything by the book, boy.
I had friends, and those with whom
I was friendly. Other ways to love never
occurred to me. Then, a ribbon of women,
one my wife for a while.
Yesterday I opened up at this, though
(I paraphrase): before I leave my body
I pray you might unite them,
that as they go about their passions
they will remain in one another
as I have remained in you Lord.
Sarah and I were smoking by the fire-pit.
It was the first time we'd tally
the relative merits of women and men, sexually:
there was the girlfriend she nearly kissed,

but for whatever reason didn't.
There was the story in which
Ruth and Naomi 'clung', their vow recited
during so many straight weddings.
There was me and my 'bromances'
and the question of whether David
ejaculated as he embraced Jonathan
as a blog I'd read that day suggested.
Is something wrong? she said,
and my fists froze in the winter cold, I mean
fixed in their sockets like branches in snowmen
and our black greyhound galloped around the garden
and my heart wet itself inside the deep
embarrassments of my body. *Of course there is.*
And my chair's wheels mark-made in the mud
and for the rest of the night we went barefoot
smoking by the inferno, throwing shit in:
twigs, leaves, paper, scraps, and reason. So then
I briefly go in the house to get my crutches, callipers,
dressings and plasters, all of my prized atrocities
and abominations, begin to throw them in too
one by one – *Of course there is* –
and everything births, ups and downs, blows out
and in, and ins and outs us. Just as I am
about to burn all of my bats and balls as well
she comes and stands above me. Jesus,
her vintage skirt of flowers, birds
and what she affectionately calls 'swirly bits',
her hair held back into a ponytail,
that black fitted tee.

Of course there is.

NOTES ON THE POEMS

fragments from **The First Week of the World:
the herpetological bible**
'Day One' and 'D( )y S( )x', an erasure poem, contain phrases
from Michael Hamburger's *The Truth of Poetry* (pp. 241-
243), which discuss Yves Bonnefoy's poem 'La Salamandre',
"occasioned by seeing a lizard on the wall of a ruined house".
Hamburger contrasts Bonnefoy's particularly French approach
to nature – "a process of self-exploration that is also a personal
search for salvation" – with that of Ted Hughes or Gerard
Manley Hopkins: "...English poetry begins with 'aspects' or
appearances whereas French poetry begins with 'essences.'"
'Day 5' is inspired by the following passage from Robbie
Hamper's *Leopard Geckos in Captivity*: "Research projects are
needed for long-term studies of Leopard Geckos in their
natural habitats, but due to environmental destruction and
civil unrest in these areas, studies are limited or non-existent."

Abnominations
Andrew Philip, in his second collection *The North End of the
Possible*, describes the abnominal this way: "The abnominal is a
form I have developed using only the letters of the dedicatee's
name, each of which must appear at least once per stanza.
The poem, which is 20 lines long, should begin and end by
addressing the dedicatee in some way. The title must also be
an anagram of their name."

Hurrah! Sober on Piranhas!
P.R.A.S stands for Portsmouth Reptile and Amphibian
Society

Jib Þrongs Jinns Sir

The Icelandic letter Þ – pronounced 'th' – has no equivalent in English. I use it 'incorrectly', with English words, to reflect the playful sonic experimentation of Sigur Ros, particularly the invented lyrical language of Volenska (or 'Hopelandic') most famously used throughout the album ( ). Effectively glossolalia, Volenska has no semantic meaning but contains sounds found in Icelandic.

Standing is the Apples to Sitting's Oranges

A poem on the theme of 'standing', performed alongside Andrew McMillan (on 'sitting') at Broadcast's 'Opposites Attract' event to launch the New Poets Festival at The Betsey Trotwood on 22nd June, 2012.

The Innocents: a found poem

Lines composed of words posted by Robert Peake on a Facebook thread I started in 2012.

Phantasmantia I: matins

Eugene Victor Tooms is the limb-stretching, liver-eating, yellow-eyed mutant in *The X-Files* episodes 'Squeeze' and 'Tooms'.

ACKNOWLEDGEMENTS:

I'm grateful to the editors of the publications in which some of these poems, or versions of them, were first published:

Silk Road Review, The Morning Star, Fit to Work: Poets Against Atos, For Rhino in a Shrinking World, Glitter is a Gender, Under the Radar, Birdbook 2: Freshwater Habitats, Poems In Which, Offi Press Mexico, Shakespeare/Austen/Bronte Project, The Poet's Quest for God, Magma, and Cake.

I'm indebted to the following for their advice and criticism on any or all of these poems: Ira Lightman, Sophie Mayer, Robert Peake, Andrew Philip, Daniel Sluman, Carrie Etter and of course, Jane Commane of Nine Arches, whose patient editorial expertise helped me turn a manuscript I was committed to into a book I could be proud of; to my parents, Lyn and Steve, for cultivating my obsession with pushing feelings, sounds and images round my plate like peas, whether with paint, music or words; to Jo, Jamie and Nikki, for being constant reminders of the creativity and courage written in our blood; to Mr. Matthews, my old school teacher, the reason I started writing; and finally to Sarah, the reason I never stopped.